Ordinary People Extraordinary Advice
PARENTING

SHARON LETOVSKY, PHD

Copyright © 2015 Sharon Letovsky, PhD

All rights reserved.

ISBN: 978-0-9868038-7-1

DEDICATION

To my parents, Rose and Julius Letovsky.
Thank you, Mom and Dad,
for everything.

PROLOGUE

We tend to underestimate our own value. We have been taught to look outside ourselves for approval. As children we look to parents, peers and teachers. Once we enter the world of work, we seek approval from bosses, colleagues, clients, customers, and the many others with whom we come into contact.

We have been taught that it is virtuous to be humble. In doing so, we often devalue what comes easily to us, and prize what others do that we cannot. We may not realize that the other person, who we think is so smart or talented, is actually admiring us.

Ordinary people are not so "ordinary". No matter what their cultural background, level of education or financial status, they have learned from the university of life. The most useful information can often come from the most unlikely of sources.

This book showcases the extraordinary advice that comes out of the mouths of ordinary people. Random people were asked the same question. "If a famous television talk-show host were to put a microphone in front of you and ask for your best one-sentence advice on parenting, what would you say?" Here are fifty of their answers.

It is fascinating that different people would have so many different responses to the same question. What shaped each answer was something that person was either dealing with right now, or had struggled with earlier in life. The question really made them think, and want to assist others who might be facing the same issues.

In this book, you will see yourself both as a parent and as an adult child to your aging parents, should you be lucky enough to still have them.

May this book give you insights to increase the happiness in your life and in the lives of those you love.

ACKNOWLEDGMENTS

To the many "not-so ordinary" people who kindly offered their extraordinary advice. Thank you for your willingness to contribute. Your thoughtful insights made this book possible.

1.

FORGIVE

"Forgive" was the very first piece of advice received for this book, and it is very well placed as number one. The person who gave this advice was a great-grandmother, aged eighty-eight, with many years' experience parenting and grand-parenting. When she spoke of forgiveness, she was referring to forgiving on multiple levels.

We have to forgive our children. They will make mistakes. They will hurt themselves, their teachers, their friends, and they will certainly hurt us. What hurts much more is holding the grudge. They may hurt us today, but if we review it multiple times in our head, we are continuing to hurt ourselves long after the hurtful event has passed. We also continue to hurt the child.

If an unpleasant event happens, deal with it, forgive and move on. Continuing to punish someone long after the event has passed is like dropping acid on the relationship. The more time passes and the longer the grudge is held, the more the relationship could deteriorate.

Forgiveness is multi-generational. Even this great-grandmother could remember things that her parents had done that were hurtful to her. How productive is it, she wondered, to keep being angry at someone, who had long since died, for something that had been done sixty-five years ago? Her father may have offended her on June 15, 1950. The next day, the event was gone, but how many days has she thought about that event since then, she reflected?

This "extraordinary" piece of advice is to forgive those you believe have wronged you; whether it is your children, parents, stepparents, grandparents, spouses, or ex-spouses. Forgiving people does not mean becoming their best friend. Forgiveness may lead to such great healing that the relationship improves exponentially. But it may not. It may not be healthy to pursue that relationship, and it may not even be possible for a variety of reasons. Forgiving may not heal the relationship, but one thing is for certain, it will heal you and enable you to move on.

2.

DON'T JUMP IN WITH ADVICE

A grandmother in her mid-sixties offered this suggestion. It seemed that what she was learning at the time was the best way to relate to her adult children and their children. Grandmothers have "been there, done that." But adult children doing their best to raise children of their own do not necessarily want to replicate the way that they were raised. Some do, but it seems that most don't. There is a natural pulling away as adult children create a home with a partner and have children together. Their value systems merge and alter to blend into a new kind of parenting that attempts to bring the best of both worlds. A change in value system can happen even if the adult child does not have a partner with which to raise the child. Adult children need to find their own way.

Jumping in with unsolicited advice can alienate adult children. They need to be able to make their own decisions. Unsolicited advice tends to backfire. The adults receiving the advice, rather than showing appreciation, can get angry and resentful. The advice can be seen as the parent not trusting them, or seeing them as smart enough to make the right decision.

But can this not also apply to teenagers, even pre-teens? Is it not then, if not earlier, that children begin to resist parental advice? Even with younger children, parents have to be strategic in how to give advice. If children experience advice as belittling or untrusting, they will become resentful. They need to see the advice as valuable, not as judgment or criticism. Then they will be more apt to listen.

3.

BE THERE FOR THEM

This advice also came from a grandmother who, over the years, had discovered that "being there for them" took different forms, and was often more challenging than one might expect. When children are little, of course we know that we need to protect them. Their physical and emotional health and safety are our top concerns. But how does "being there for them" change as they get older?

There was a time when "the teacher was always right". If children got into trouble at school, they could expect further trouble at home. Now the situation is different. The hierarchical, authoritarian old-school days are past. Parents defend their children. Maintaining the balance between being there for them and teaching them right from wrong is a delicate one. Too much "parenting" can alienate them and drive their behavior underground, where parents can neither see nor deal with it. Be there for them, but remember who is the parent, and develop forms other than authoritarian ones like "because I say so" as your methods of communication. Most importantly, keep the lines of communication open.

With adult children, being there for them is equally challenging yet different. The grandmother who contributed this idea was struggling with this issue. Her actual suggestion was: "Be there for them, so they know you are there for them". Adult children are raising their own families and often reject parental support as well as advice. If they ask you to babysit, they will worry that you may not do it properly. Any suggestions can be perceived as advice giving, treating them like children and therefore rejected. How do you be there for them if they do not want it? Even more challenging is how to be there for them if they seem to neither value nor respect you. Adult children are very busy with their own families, and are often overwhelmed. Your offers of help can actually feel draining.

The simple answer, yet not so easy to implement, is a combination of accepting and adapting to their stage of life, and patience. Be there for them no matter what. Even if it feels they don't want or need you, they actually do!

4.

TEACH THEM TO BE RESPONSIBLE

The umbilical cord is cut when the child is born, but is it really? The psychological umbilical cord is there for life; and it is thousands of little strings all bound into one. When do we start teaching responsibility? We cut those thousands of strings one at a time, slowly, throughout their lives.

Some experts will tell you that giving children responsibility early is good for them. It teaches them to think for themselves. Others will tell you to wait. Giving children responsibility before their time puts too heavy a burden on their young shoulders. There is no magic age. The only thing you can be sure of is that, no matter which way you turn, someone will have something to say about it.

So much depends on the individual child's personality and level of skill. Even in the same family, giving different children the same responsibilities at certain set ages may work in some families but not in others. It is important to respect the children's individual differences, and not chastise them for not being exactly like their brother or sister. For example, one child may be well organized and perfectly capable of doing his or her own laundry at a certain age, while another might be a complete disaster at it. Another child might be able to handle money well, and be able to deal with a larger allowance that allows for saving and purchase of more expensive items, while a sibling may need more time to develop that skill.

Working with the child's interest, personality and skill, and encouraging and facilitating more responsibility in those areas is the best way to proceed. One child may be interested in what goes on in the kitchen, while another may be more fascinated by mechanical things. Children who love nature can help out in the garden, and perhaps even have their own corner. Children who love playing school can be responsible for other children. And the mechanical child can help change a light bulb or hold the wrench while you fix the faucet. The technique of following a child's personality, interests and skill when developing responsibility ensures that they embrace responsibility with enthusiasm rather than resentment.

5.

TEACH THEM TO BE ACCOUNTABLE

The person who suggested that we teach children to be responsible also mentioned the word accountable in the same sentence. The two words are often used interchangeably, but their meanings are quite different and worth exploring when it comes to parenting.

Responsibility implies "dependability", yet accountability means "answerability". A child may be responsible for doing the dishes, but the child is accountable for their cleanliness. The two words are intertwined and one leads to the other.

Responsibility without accountability is hollow. Whether the child is responsible for babysitting, mowing the lawn, doing the dishes or cooking dinner, accountability implies that the child must not only do the job, but do the job well or be answerable for the consequences. Accountability implies follow-through and reinforces the sense of responsibility. But how does one teach accountability?

When giving children responsibilities, or allowing them to assume responsibility for things they want to be responsible for, it is important to work with the child to define what constitutes a job well done. If they assume responsibility for a certain thing, what are they answerable for? For example, doing the dishes means different things in different households. In one household, it means loading the dishwasher. In another household, the dishes are not considered "done" unless, in addition to loading the dishwasher, the sink and counters are washed and clear and the floor is swept.

Know what it is that you expect and ensure that the child knows it too. Then, when they assume responsibility for something, they will have a yardstick against which to measure their success.

6.

LISTEN TO THEM

Listening is not a passive activity. Many people think they can type on their smartphone or computer or otherwise do something else while they are supposedly listening. They believe they are multi-tasking. Indeed they may think they are able to give one hundred percent attention to two different things at the same time, but we all know that is not the case. They may be hearing what the other person is saying, but they are not actually listening. So what is the difference, and how does this affect your children?

How do you feel when you are talking to someone and they are typing or reading an email? Most people feel as if they are not being listened to. They become confused, repeat themselves, forget their train of thought, and for these reasons go on talking longer than they had intended, because they forget where they were going. They then either turn off or get angry. Sound familiar?

Close your eyes for a moment and pay attention to the ambient sounds around you. Perhaps you can hear the fan from the heating or cooling system, or the noise from outside your window. People do their best to block out these sounds when concentrating on something. They can hear them, but are not listening to them.

It is important to hear the words your children are saying as more than ambient sounds in the background. Stop what you are doing, and give them your full attention. They will probably only take a moment or two of your time. If you are in the middle of doing something important, tell them so. Ask them if it is urgent, and if it is not, tell them you will give them your full attention when you are finished. Then make sure you fulfill your promise!

Listening actively to your children has multiple advantages. First, they feel respected and valued. Second, their words and feelings give you valuable insight into their lives; what is going on for them and how they are experiencing it. Listening to them can help you to help them solve problems and even prevent problems before they happen.

Listening is absolutely your most valuable tool for influencing your children. When you listen, you are receiving valuable data that you can later use. They are showing you what they value, what is important to them. When you want to influence them to do something at a later date, rather than "commanding" them as you might a young child, use the information you have gathered to show how doing what you want resonates with their values.

7.

LET THEM KNOW THAT THEY CAN COME TO YOU

Where can children of any age go when they have a problem? Parents usually want their children to come to them before going anywhere else. That means that parents have to be willing and able to deal with the difficult issues that children, especially teens and adult children, bring to the door. Sometimes these issues can challenge parents' values and belief systems.

What if your teenager wants to become intimate with her boyfriend and needs birth control? Could she discuss this with you? Would you become angry and judgmental and try to keep the boy away? If so, what would this do to your relationship with her? Perhaps she would listen to you and break up with the boyfriend, but what do you think the odds are for that outcome? More likely she would go to another source, perhaps a clinic, for the medication, or perhaps she would take a chance and not use birth control. Then you could wind up with a much bigger problem!

Whether children these days are facing more problems today than years ago, or whether we are just hearing more about them, the challenge is the same. Children can unfortunately face problems with addiction, sex, pregnancy, eating disorders, bullying, harassment and much more. Adult children are no different, except add marital and child rearing problems into the mix. Parents want their children to be able to come to them to help solve these problems. How parents respond is crucial.

Being able to be there for your children, no matter what is going on in their lives, means not losing your cool when you get whacked with something that challenges your values and beliefs. It is important to remember two things: first, that you are not at fault for the problem and second, that you are responsible for your reaction to the news.

Be nice. The child is in pain. Here is a true example. A fifteen-year-old, while in the car with her mother, turned to her mother and said, "Mom, I joined AA (Alcoholics Anonymous)." The mom was shocked and did not know what to say. She was torn between yelling at the child for drinking, congratulating her child for joining AA, and feeling guilty for not knowing that the child even had a problem. What would you do?

The mother gripped the steering wheel, took a deep breath and congratulated the child for joining AA. Then she apologized for not knowing about the drinking and not being there for the child. The teenager then surprised her mother with this very adult response: "You *were* there for me. That is why I can kick it and come to you when I am fifteen and not when I am fifty."

Be there, no matter what. It can be difficult, but it works!

8.

LOVE THEM, NO MATTER WHAT

A few people from different age brackets and walks of life mentioned "Love them". Parents with young children admitted that there were times when it was difficult to love their children. Parents with older children and grandchildren said the same. There were times when children, at various ages, behaved in ways that made it very hard for the parent to love the child.

A mother of a seven year old, struggling with a willful child, said, "If I say wear your pink socks, she will wear her blue ones, just to aggravate me. There are days when I want to strangle her." A parent of a thirty-something-year old, who is much taller and stronger than she is, spoke of her fear when he yells at her for having been an "awful parent." And a grandmother, hearing of how her adult granddaughter is behaving, had difficulty understanding how the mother could continue to love the child through that behavior.

The advice was not only to love them, but also to "love them even when you don't want to, when it doesn't come naturally." A thirty-four-year-old woman, whose father has not spoken with her for many years, brought this idea home. Even though she has tried to mend fences, she says he will not forgive her for what he says she "put him through" when she was a child. Interestingly, this women presents as a strong, confident, intelligent, educated woman, who is making a valuable contribution to her community and society at large, both through her writing and work with disadvantaged adults. One cannot imagine that a parent would not be proud of such a child.

Certainly there may be individual instances when parents feel frustrated, angry, hurt, ashamed, disappointed, or many other things about their children. This piece of advice is meant to remind you to cut your kids some slack, no matter what their ages. They are going through life's challenges, perhaps just as you did at their age, and they are dealing with them the best way they can. Sometimes that means either distancing themselves from their parents, or using parents as a "safe" target for their pent-up frustrations.

Do not put yourself in danger. If you fear for your safety, either emotionally or physically, from an abusive child, protect yourself and give yourself some distance. This advice is to love them anyway, and allow their light to shine through the periods of darkness. Allow them to come around, even if it takes a while.

9.

BUILD CONFIDENCE

People agreed with the idea that parents need to build their children's confidence. Others said parents need to develop their children's sense of accomplishment and still others referred to building self-esteem. The question then arose, "What differentiates the three?"

Further discussion uncovered that parents' idea of confidence had to do with the child's being good in one thing, an individual activity in which the child could feel capable and be praised. For example, let us look at Joshua. At this writing, Joshua is twelve years old. His early school years had been a little problematic. Because of fine motor problems, he struggled with learning to write. On the playing field, he was also a little clumsier than most and could not catch a ball.

But Joshua's parents persisted with his homework, and soon noticed that he was a whiz at math and computers. Wanting to expand his horizons beyond the computer screen, while other parents may have given up on athletics, Joshua's parents encouraged him to try different sports, both individual and group, until he found his niche. Who could have predicted that, a few short years later, Joshua would be on a competitive curling team that placed third in the city?

Another child, Sarah, struggled with learning disabilities that affected every area of her life. Sarah's mother, struggling to find a way to develop Sarah's confidence, began to observe Sarah's natural talents. Sarah had quick reflexes and was a great problem solver. Mom experimented by asking Sarah to hold the wrench while she fixed the faucet, or pass her a new light bulb when the previous one was burned out.

Sarah, at the tender age of nine, became the official "Mister Fix-it" at home. Did Mom really need a nine-year-old Mister Fix-it? Of course not!

But she breathed a sigh of relief as she saw little Sarah's chest puff up with pride as she developed newfound confidence in her special role. This confidence in something she could do well not only helped Sarah survive that difficult time, but also sustained her through many challenging years ahead.

10.

GIVE THEM A SENSE OF ACCOMPLISHMENT

Joshua and Sarah developed confidence when they realized that they were good at something. But acquiring a sense of accomplishment requires measurable results. When Joshua played a good game with his curling team, he hopefully felt confident in his playing ability, but he got a sense of accomplishment from his team's good performance. He may have been confident in his mathematical ability, but he got a sense of accomplishment from solving challenging problems. Sarah felt confident in her ability to help mom fix things, but she got a sense of accomplishment when the faucet no longer leaked, or the new light fixture was installed.

Children need both confidence and a sense of accomplishment. It is not enough for them to know they are good at something, they also need to see the benefits of that ability. They need feedback. They need to see results.

Confidence without sense of accomplishment is hollow. Children are often smarter than we think. They see through any false praise, any confidence-boosting attempts that are not backed up with tangible evidence. That evidence may be difficult to find, especially if the child is struggling, but find it you must. A sense of accomplishment turns the confidence that you worked so hard to build into something that can last.

11.

BUILD SELF-ESTEEM

Many of us are taught that pride is a sin and it is important to be humble. But what does that mean? We want our children to be proud of themselves, of their capabilities and their accomplishments. We want them to grow up feeling good in their own skin, rather than ashamed and humiliated. So how does a parent find the right balance between self-esteem and arrogance? Where is the tipping point?

Self-esteem does not come from the feeling that the child knows everything or is better than others. Even if the child is very accomplished in a certain area, self-esteem comes from the experience of success; from capability, supported by tangible accomplishments. This allows the child to feel good, to be able to look in the mirror and say, "I am a somebody."

Now we are at the tipping point. When this looking in the mirror is transferred outward and becomes, "I am better than you" or "No one can tell me what to do because I am the best", then the ability has converted to arrogance and pride, in the negative sense of the world.

It is quite fine, even necessary, for children to feel proud of themselves, and it is especially nice to feel proud of our children. Self-esteem comes when this pride is internal rather than external. It is a deep sense of feeling good about who they are, not that they have finished learning and growing, but that they are doing fine and are well on their way.

12.

TEACH THEM HOW TO LEARN

People saw openness to learning as something very important to teach children. They were not referring only to what children learn in school, they were talking about the ability to acquire and retain new information. People recognized that the basics of how to read, write and do mathematics are only the tip of the iceberg. The desire to acquire advanced or deeper learning on any subject must come from within, and this needs to be nourished. Children need to become self-directed learners.

This goes back to the earlier discussion on helping children find their niche. If Joshua shows an aptitude for mathematics, it is important to put Joshua into situations where he can learn more about what he loves. This is particularly important if the child shows aptitude in area in which you are not proficient. Encourage the child to be curious about what he or she loves. Open the door to the child's wanting to know as much as possible, and create the situations in which this can happen.

Once the spark catches, as it did with Joshua when he reached the age of around ten, children will take that desire to learn more about the subject and create those situations for themselves. They will become self-directed learners, and this is a skill that will stand them in good stead for the rest of their lives.

13.

ENCOURAGE THEM TO BE SMARTER THAN YOU ARE

This is a tough one. We equip our children with everything we can, then we send them off into the world to make their way. Khalil Gibran, in his book, *The Prophet*, has a poem about children. He likens parents to a bow and children to arrows. A bow sets the arrow's trajectory, but cannot follow it. If the bow did not release the arrow, it could not fly. Or if the bow released the arrow gently but tried to hang on, the arrow would fall to the ground. Parents need to set the trajectory and let go. The question is, when is that okay?

It can be scary for parents to see their children becoming smarter or more knowledgeable than they are. When children are very young, parents are the "big shots". They know everything, and control their children's lives to a great extent. As children get older, parents need to slowly begin to release that control. The timing and degree of that letting go can be difficult to ascertain. How much control do parents release, and when? Seeing their children get into areas parents do not understand can make parents feel fearful and insecure.

The challenge in encouraging your children to be smarter than you are is more about you than about them. It is about letting go of your fear and insecurity and allowing your arrows to soar. You cannot be with them every day of their lives. You have to trust that you have set them on a good trajectory, that you have taught them the values, morals and principles that they need to guide their lives. Let go, and help them to fly.

14.

DON'T LIE TO THEM

Some people interviewed for this book spoke of family "secrets", of things from which they felt they had to protect their children. Others spoke of family secrets from which they, themselves, had been protected. These people advise parents to tell children the truth. "Children are much more savvy than we realize", they said. Children know something is going on. If you do not tell them what that "something" is, they will sense it anyway. They will not know how to behave in situations involving that person or thing that is at the bottom of the issue you are keeping from them. There is also the potential that they may imagine the situation is far worse than it actually is. In the long term, these people said, the children will hold it against you.

One grandmother shared this example. She was having a problem with her daughter, a young mother of three. Each felt hurt by the other over a situation that had happened a couple of months previously. The older woman wanted to make amends, put the situation behind them, and move forward, but her daughter, the young mother, felt too hurt to do so just yet.

The daughter told her mother that she was not discussing the incident with the children and requested that her mother not do so either.

Unexpectedly, the mother, grandmother and grandchildren found themselves together at a family gathering. When the grandchildren saw their grandmother, instead of rushing over with big hugs, as they would have done previously, they appeared stunned. They did not know whether to approach their grandmother or not, and when they did, they were tentative. They behaved like strangers.

Although their mother is keeping the original situation a secret from them, the children have ears. They overhear mother and father discussing it at home. They no longer feel free to behave as they wish with their grandmother. In addition, who knows what they may have created in their imagination?

Children know that something is "up" when there is a family secret. It is best for all concerned to see if you can find a comfortable way to at least give them some information about what is going on.

15.

FEEL GOOD ABOUT YOURSELF

We all talk to ourselves, and most self-talk is negative. These criticisms can be positive if they push us to improve, but most of the time they just make us feel miserable. Self-doubt is contagious. If you do not feel good about yourself, how can you expect your children to feel good about themselves? They are leaning on you, so it is important to set a positive example.

This is not to say that you should lie to yourself, or pretend that you have knowledge and skill that you do not have. Of course you always want to be learning and developing yourself. Most people, however, make themselves miserable by lingering over yesterday and fretting about tomorrow. You cannot change yesterday, and tomorrow is not governed by your fears. It is governed by the choices you make today.

The best way to feel good about yourself is to focus on today. You do that by trusting the decisions that you made in the past. Of course when you look backwards in time, you may have regrets. You have more information today than you did at the time. When you made those past decisions, you did not wake up in the morning and decide to make mistakes. You made the best decision possible given the information you had. You now have different, new information. So make a new decision. Fix what may have been broken in the past.

The decisions you make daily, hourly, even minute-to-minute set your course and create your future. Your job is not to be a great Nelson Mandela or Dalai Lama. Your job is to be the best "you" that you can be. Your children do not need Nelson Mandela; they need you.

16.

TEACH THEM TO BE COURAGEOUS

We all want our children to be safe, so we tell them to look both ways when they cross the street and to not talk with strangers. As they get older, we guide them to have the kinds of friends we value and to avoid trouble. But how can we teach courage?

People cannot grow unless they are willing to step into the unknown, and parents must teach this to their children. Children need to know that, although they cannot know all the potential outcomes of all situations, they can know some. Knowing just enough and moving forward is where courage lies. It is in the space between recklessness and fear.

Courage is best taught one step at a time. But the important thing to remember is that, in order to teach children to be less fearful and more courageous, you first have to feel less fearful and more courageous yourself.

A grandmother described how she taught her grandson to ride a bicycle. The child's father had spent most of the afternoon holding onto the back of the bicycle seat and running alongside while little Jonathan rode around the block. Exhausted and spent, Dad and son had just come into the house for a drink when Grandma arrived.

Grandma asked Jonathan to show her his new bicycle. While Dad had kept to the sidewalk in order to stay safe, Grandma took Jonathan to the empty parking lot across the street. Perhaps, she thought, Jonathan would feel less constrained there. They started at one end of the lot, with Grandma holding onto the seat as Dad had done. Noticing, after only a short distance, that Jonathan had good balance, she let go. Jonathan rode all the way to the other end of the parking lot, then stopped and turned around to look up at Grandma. But she was not there. She was way back where they had started from, at the other end of the parking lot. Jonathan was flabbergasted! And the rest, as they say, is history.

Was it just that Jonathan had practiced enough with Dad and was ready to ride, or was there another factor? With Grandma, there was a little more freedom, and a little more risk-taking. Jonathan had the space to go faster, and Grandma had the willingness to let go. There was space for both of them to be more courageous.

Of course there is much more to life than learning to ride a bicycle, but the same principle applies in other situations. Gather you own courage, push your eaglets a little bit, and encourage them to fly.

17.

TEACH THEM RESPECT

Various people advised teaching children respect. They were parents of teens, parents of married children and even people with no children at all.

They saw today's concern with teaching children self-confidence and self-esteem as a double-edged sword. They were concerned that respect for parents and other adults could be getting lost in the process.

They lamented that there was a time when children stood when adults entered a room, and when teenagers on crowded public transit actually gave up their seats for adults.

The people who advised teaching children respect did not want to sound like their parents or grandparents (and some of them admitted that they did, indeed, feel a bit like echoes). They did not want a return to what some of them had experienced as the excessively strict days of their youth. They were advocating balance.

There was a fear that some parents are so concerned with respecting their children that they forget to teach the children to respect their parents. The people who suggested this advice were feeling that lack of respect from their older children, and it hurt. They wanted to spare younger parents that pain.

Respect your children, and teach them self-respect, but do not tolerate their disrespect for you. Obedience and respect are two different things. They would be very interesting children (and perhaps not from this planet) if they obeyed your every word. But even if they do not obey, it is important to not tolerate disrespect. If you tolerate it once, then twice, then three times, their disrespect for you will become a habit that could be very difficult to break later.

18.

AVOID LABELING YOUR CHILD AS "SHY"

Surely we have all been out and about when we encountered a friend or acquaintance, a parent accompanied by a young child who buries his or her head in the parent's clothing and refuses to greet us when introduced. The parent may ask the child to say hello, but when the child burrows further into the parent's leg, the parent then adds, "He's so shy!" This label provides the child with an excuse. The child no longer has to obey the parent's request to greet us. The person giving this advice warned that the "shy" label not only gives the child an excuse to be rude, it can actually stick and even hamper the child later.

Of course children are shy. They begin to "make shy" at the age of seven months, when they first realize that some of those big people out there are not Mommy or Daddy. They are rightfully scared. It is a big world, and their natural shyness is a built-in defense mechanism.

Virtually as soon as children can comprehend words, parents warn them to be wary of strangers. And then parents are surprised when they bury their little heads in Mommy or Daddy's clothing when they are out and about and encounter someone they do not know.

What can parents do to help children be less shy? One option is to identify the person as known to Mommy and Daddy and not a stranger. Another option is to prepare the child in advance. Practice at home before going out in public. Teach them the proper behavior when encountering a stranger. Children can be taught to shake hands and say "hello" as adults do.

Some children, however, really are very shy. They can clam up when encountering people they do not know. These children need more practice and reassurance. Do not force a very shy child to greet someone who is a stranger to them if they are really frightened. Excuse them by saying something like, "perhaps next time", but avoid labeling the child. Once the child feels identified as a "shy" person, the child can begin to adopt more shy behaviors, and this could cause them problems later.

19.

RECOGNIZE AND HONOR BOTH INTROVERTS AND EXTROVERTS

We used to think that introversion was about being shy and extroversion was about being outgoing, but the definition goes much deeper than that. Extroverts are comfortable in groups of people. They get energy from others and their energy level rises the more time they spend with people. For example, at a dinner party, the extrovert will get more energy as the evening progresses. In a meeting, the extrovert will be the one speaking up.

Introverts on the other hand are drained by groups of people and prefer their interactions one-on-one. At a party, you will see them sitting in a quiet corner with one or two other people. At a meeting, they will listen intently, speaking up very little or not at all. Their best ideas come to them after the meeting, when they are back at their desks.

Unfortunately, our society seems to prize extroverts. The introvert child is the one who will appear shy, while the extrovert will be happily chatting and perhaps performing for others, even strangers.

Introversion and extroversion are personality types. People are born one type or the other, and do not change much throughout their lives. The introvert can learn to be more outspoken and the extrovert can learn to tone down and not monopolize meetings, but it is important to recognize that you can no more convert an introvert child into an extrovert than you can change eye color.

Parents need to honor both types in their children. Introverts need time alone to recharge their batteries. They also need time to cogitate. They may not have the fast answers that extroverts do, but they often have better answers. Be patient.

Extroverts can appear more boisterous and can speak before they think. They need our patience too. They can be performers and actors. Parents need to honor who they are, and work with their strengths, channeling their outgoing energy in positive ways rather than trying to make them into something different.

20.

DON'T ABDICATE

Experts advise new parents to, rather than say no to a child, give the child a choice. For example, if it is a chilly day outside and the child does not want to wear a coat, say, for example, "Do you want to wear your red coat or your fluffy green one? (i.e., "no coat" is not an option). It can be difficult to know when, as a parent, one is taking this "give the child a choice" advice a bit too far.

At what age are children capable of making what kinds of decisions? It is important to not abdicate your decision-making to a three-year-old. First of all, it denigrates your own authority and second, it puts on the shoulders of the child a responsibility for which the child is not capable. It is difficult to find the balance between discipline and breaking the child's spirit. Sometimes it can be hard to believe that three year-olds can learn to sit quietly in a restaurant, eat with a knife and fork (albeit poorly) and use a napkin. But they can.

The person who suggested parents not abdicate their authority spoke of sitting in a restaurant watching a parent with a child who was absolutely uncontrollable. The parent kept saying, "Sit down, okay?" as if she were asking the child permission. Apparently it was not okay with the child to sit down, since he kept running around.

There are times for choice and times for authority. Finding the balance is one of the key challenges of parenting, one that helps you be respected and honored in your child's eyes. Teach you child to make decisions, yet maintain your authority and your child's respect.

21.

BE AN AUTHORITY VS. AUTHORITARIAN

The two words authority and authoritarian seem similar but they have very different meanings. An *authority* is someone who knows more about a certain subject than the average person. People would go to this person for information or advice. The word *authoritarian*, however, refers to style rather than knowledge. Someone who is authoritarian has a command and control style, much like a dictator.

When the child is very young, the parent needs to be both an authority and authoritarian. The child cannot make decisions about whether or not to play with that knife or touch the lamp. The parent makes those decisions for the child. There are clear "no's".

As the child gets older, however, being authoritarian, that is, telling the child what to do or not to do, works increasingly less. Parents need to rely more on their knowledge and experience than on giving orders. As children hit their teenage years, they will often not obey, or worse, they will pretend to obey and go underground. If they fear you, they will not confide in you. You then run the risk of their getting into terrible trouble and not telling you until it is too late.

Establish your authority over time, as you transition slowly from being authoritarian to being an authority. Demonstrate your knowledge and skill to the child, through your actions and behaviors. If you take time and care with this transition, your children will "see" that you are an authority. You will not have to "tell" them.

22.

MEAN IT

If your dog soils the carpet and you do nothing, what do you think will happen tomorrow? If you said the dog would soil the carpet again, you are correct. If you have a rule for your pet and you do not enforce it, there is no point having the rule in the first place.

So it is with rules, and particularly with threats, when it comes to your children. Do not bother making a rule if you have no plans to enforce it, or indeed, if the rule is unenforceable. Threats are even more challenging to enforce than rules. This is because when people make a threat, they are usually upset. A parent might say, for example, "If you don't stop doing that there will be no screen time for a week!" Really? No screen time for a week? Impossible. Madison, who is only seven years old and in second grade, receives her math assignments via email. Can't even do her homework without screen time. And how would you stop her from looking at her favorite cute kitten video on YouTube while she's doing her math up in her room?

So what happens to Mom's authority if little Madison does something Mommy does not like, then Mommy makes a threat, and little Madison subverts that threat? Little Madison has pulled a fast one on Mommy.

Madison is a good kid, but she is just a kid and she will do what kids do. So take a moment and cool your jets before you make any threat. If it is unenforceable, it will do your authority more harm than good. If you have a rule and make a threat should that rule be broken, make sure it is a threat that you are capable of and prepared to carry out. This will help you maintain both your authority and your child's respect.

23.

BE A PARENT, NOT A FRIEND

As children mature, parents may want to become friends with them. This can be tempting, but it can backfire on you later. They may resent you for not having been a "parent" to them. It's a paradox. Children rail against your authority, but they can end up resenting you if they later think that you didn't provide enough.

Divorced parents are particularly vulnerable to this paradox. When there are two parents in a home, there is a natural hierarchy. The parents are on top, the children below. When there is only one parent, the hierarchy tends to flatten and the family unit becomes a team, with the parent as team lead, a position very different from that of owner or president. In a multiple child home, the single parent is outnumbered so decision-making becomes more collaborative. All of this may lead parent and children to see themselves as equals. It may also encourage the parent to share personal issues with the children and seek their advice, thus reversing the natural way of things.

Befriending ones own children happens in two-parent homes as well. As a child matures, a parent may feel particularly close to one child and begin to treat that child as a friend and confide things that perhaps the child has no business knowing. This could put increased burden on the child. The parent should be caring for the child, not the other way around.

So don't try to be a friend to your own children. Get your own friends. They are the ones in whom you can be confiding and from whom you may want to seek advice or input. Love your children, guide and protect them, and encourage them to leave the nest and soar. But remember, you are the parent and they are your children. They are not your friends.

24.

DON'T PRY

As children get older, parents cannot know everything that is happening in their children's lives. Children have their secrets, and parents have theirs. But how can parents ensure that they are being informed of the important issues in their children's lives and could protect them, or at least be there for them, if things were to go terribly wrong?

The answer to this question lies in the difference between pushing and allowing. When people push you for information that you are not ready to share, how does it feel? If you said "uncomfortable", you are absolutely right. Adults do not like to be pushed for information, and neither do children. When pushed, children can clam up.

The secret answer lies in three key words: safety, trust and openness. Your children will come to you with important issues in their lives only if they feel safe. If they are afraid of your reaction, or of losing your approval, they will protect themselves and you from that information, and they will not share.

They must also trust you. They must trust that you will behave consistently with their expectations of you; that is, that you will not surprise them, and that you will have their best interests at heart.

Last, there must be a climate of openness in the family. If you family has a more private style, in which people do not speak of personal issues, it would be inconsistent with family norms for your child to divulge things you may not want to hear. Whereas, if you work to create a climate in which personal issues are discussed, then you children will be more inclined to come and share information with you. There will be no need to pry.

25.

TELL THEM WHEN THEY DO SOMETHING RIGHT

It is the parents' job to correct their children when they do things wrong, or when they forget to do things that they know they should do. But it is important to pay attention to the relative percentage of negative versus positive comments in the household.

Most parents do not even notice how often they correct their children. It takes an outsider to notice it, and if the outsider were to comment on it, you can be sure the parent would object.

A grandparent was visiting her daughter and grandchildren. During the first half-hour of the visit, she heard her daughter correcting one of the grandchildren five different times. The daughter meant well, and was probably trying to show her mother what a conscientious parent she was. The grandmother did not dare to say anything at the time, but she did share the incident when providing advice for this book.

The next time you find yourself alone with your children, keep an open notebook handy and observe yourself. Count how many times in a half-hour period you correct your children, or tell them to do something. Then count how many times you compliment them on something they have done well. If you are like most parents, you will probably see that the number is heavily weighted on the negative side.

Challenge yourself, over the next little while, to consciously reverse the weighting, so that the positive comments outnumber the negative ones.

26.

BE GENUINE

It means a lot to your children when you compliment them on a job well done. Some parents take this advice to heart and compliment their children excessively. This is great when your child merits the compliments, but remember that children, even very young ones, are smarter than adults sometimes think. Children can recognize a false compliment a mile away.

Compliment your children when they deserve it, but do not compliment them when they do not. They will see through the compliment and disregard it. They can then begin to disregard the genuine compliments that you give them, too, disbelieving them as well.

Being genuine boosts your credibility with your children. They will know that they can trust what you say. If you tell them you are proud of them, they will know that you are sincere and it will mean more to them. They will strive to earn your compliments and this will increase their respect for themselves as well as for you.

27.

EMPOWER THEM

When we do things for others that they can do for themselves, we disempower them. This applies to people of all ages, even very young children.

People tend to underestimate what their children can do. They disempower their children by doing too much for them, giving too much advice, telling them what to do, and worrying about them constantly, even after they have become adults.

Parents can inadvertently disempower their children through over-protection. A young man told of working as a medical student in a hospital in northern Canada. Fist nations people who were living way up north off the land would often bring in children, aged about four, whose legs were not developing properly. The doctors investigated diets, potential congenital or hormonal defects and many other possible causes.

The doctors then discovered that mothers usually carried their babies on their backs in a tikinagan (cradleboard), a traditional kind of baby carrier. The child was swaddled (wrapped tightly in a small blanket) and strapped to a specially designed flat board, usually made of a wood plank, then covered with beautifully decorated animal skins. These children were being carried, even to the age of four, to protect them, but they were not learning to walk.

In modern society parents can also overprotect their children by doing too much for them, things they could be doing for themselves.

The greatest scientific discoveries are made through trial and error. This is incorporated into the education system as "the discovery method". Empowering children means allowing them to use the discovery method as much as possible at home, too.

28.

GET THEM TO DO CHORES

People interviewed for this book advised that children be given chores as soon as they could understand the concept. Things like putting away toys before dinner and keeping one's room tidy are the obvious ones, but more significant chores can start earlier than one might think.

Who cleans up after dinner? Perhaps that is the time for parents to exit the room and leave it to one or more of the children to clean up. Children as young as five can learn to load a dishwasher (except for dangerous items like sharp knives). Children as young as five can also learn to fold and put away laundry. Children by the age of ten can even learn how to use a washing machine and clothes dryer. None of these are rocket science. They have the advantage of giving the children something that is uniquely theirs, which they can be responsible for, do well, and be proud of. It gives them the opportunity to contribute.

It is important to remember to teach the children to do the chore correctly, that is, according to family (read parental) standards. Take the time to teach the child how you want the chore done, for example, how the dishwasher is to be loaded or how the laundry is to be folded. And follow-up. Do not get angry every time they do a chore only halfway. Call them back and show them what you want. If you are consistent with your follow-up, after only a few times, they will know what to do. If you are inconsistent, they will do it to their own standard, which may not be yours, and you will be frustrated every time.

In certain cases, the child may be incapable of doing the chore to your standards, and you may have to lower the bar for the time being. Choose your battles. Your relationship is more important than the chore.

29.

LET THEM MAKE THEIR OWN CHOICES, BUT GUIDE THEM

People tell stories of having been forced into doing certain things, like taking piano lessons, for example, and hating piano for the rest of their lives. Others spoke of hating playing piano at first, then learning to love it, and it sustaining them throughout their lives. So what is the secret? How can you know when to guide your children's choices or let them choose for themselves? The best answer involves a combination of balance, listening and respect.

There has to be a balance between what you think is correct for your child and the child's ability to choose. Let use one family as an example. The family has a backyard pool, so the children have no choice about whether or not to take swimming lessons. The family values music, so piano lessons are also compulsory. The children then get to choose one other activity for themselves.

Another way of interpreting balance between your choices and theirs is to set time frames. For example, if a child wants to try gymnastics or karate, some parents may say, "Okay, but whatever you choose, you have to do it for one full year, so choose carefully." That gives the child an opportunity to get a solid taste of the activity before deciding whether or not to give it up. It also teaches children to be responsible for their choices.

Listening and respect are also important in determining whether to let your children make their own choices. One woman told of how piano lessons were terribly unpleasant for her as a child. Even though she had five years of lessons, their value to her was as if she had done one year, five times over. Why? Because playing piano did not fit her personality. Piano lessons involved structure and order, which made her feel trapped. Although she was musical, she was more creative than structured. At ten, she picked up a guitar, taught herself to play and made a career out of it; however, she still cannot sit at a piano for more than five minutes without wanting to get up and run away.

Sometimes you may think that a choice you have made for your child is very important, but it is important to pay attention if that choice is causing the child pain. You may not agree that piano lessons are painful, especially if you are working hard and paying good money for them. That is where respect comes in. Your children are not you. They will see things differently and they will approach problems differently. You may like structure and order, whereas you child may be creative and feel constrained by structure. The reverse could also be true.

Listen to them. If a choice you have made for them is truly painful, perhaps set a minimum time frame so they at least give it a good try. If they are still suffering after the time period has elapsed, respect who they are and let them move on.

30.

PUT THEIR NEEDS FIRST

Parents of very young children often have no choice but to put the children's needs first. A baby crying in the middle of the night needs to be fed, whether the parent feels like getting up or not. Toddlers crying because they fell and hurt themselves or are tired or hungry need parental attention, and it doesn't matter if mother is in the bathroom or on an important phone call. When children are young, even taking a shower can become an event that requires planning!

As children get older, parents may find themselves spending their early mornings or evenings driving children to activities, while juggling their own work as well as home chores. So at this age, too, there is no doubt that children's needs often come first.

Parenting seems to take forever, but when grandparents look back, they say that it was only intense for ten or twelve years. "Ten or twelve years?" you may say, "That's forever!" because it does feel like forever at the time. But from the perspective of a sixty-five-year-old, ten years is a very short period. In the big scheme of things, you have a very short window to really be there for your children. Once they hit their later teens, they really do not need you at their beck and call any longer.

Putting their needs first means skip the meeting and go to your child's hockey game. Perhaps the child won't be playing next year. Reschedule the appointment and go to your daughter's dance recital. She may not be dancing next year. The window to actually put your children's needs first may feel as if it will go on forever and drain you dry. At the time, it is not easy to remember that there are many, many years left of your life after the children are grown and gone. If you live the current normal life span, after your children hit twenty, you will have sixty plus years of life to do whatever you want.

Enjoy their childhood years as much as you can. Be there for them. Attend their activities and play with them, whether it is baseball, hockey, singing, dancing, or video games. Do whatever you and your children do and love together. You only need to put their needs first for a short while.

31.

TAKE GOOD CARE OF YOURSELF

A certain song, written in 1928, can sometimes still be heard today. It was even used in a videogame as recently as 2013. The chorus goes like this: "Button up your overcoat, when the wind is free. Take good care of yourself, you belong to me."

Parents should put their children's needs first, but parents must also find ways to keep their own cup full at the same time. Raising children requires time and energy, and can be very draining. It can even make people's resistance so low that they become sick. Parenting takes its toll physically, mentally and emotionally.

Pay attention to yourself! What is your physical health like? Have you gained or lost weight? Is your energy low? If so, don't ignore it, do something! A good parent is a healthy parent. If you are exhausted all the time, it may be because of that extra weight or perhaps an allergy to something in your diet. If not for yourself, do it for your children. They deserve a parent with energy!

If you are mentally or emotionally exhausted, get to the bottom of it. Do not grin and bear it. Your immune system knows if you are mentally and emotionally exhausted and it does not function well under those circumstances. Going to speak with a psychologist or joining a support group is not shameful. It is interesting that people will not resist going to the doctor if they have a broken arm, but if the hurt is mental or emotional, they expect to be able to fix it themselves.

Culture teaches us that it is bad to be selfish. Self-care is not selfishness. Self-care is a requirement beyond parenting. It is a requirement for living!

32.

GET THEM TO PLAY OUTSIDE

The grandmother who suggested this advice was lamenting that her grandchildren spend too much time in front of a computer screen. Whether they are playing games, watching videos or even looking things up on the Internet, they never seemed to play outside "as we did in our day". She wished they would go ride their bicycles, play sports, or even go collect bugs in a jar. "Where were the old days?" she lamented. That grandmother did not realize how right she was.

Researchers led by Ian Morgan of Australian National University recently reported in the medical journal, Lancet, that up to 90% of young adults in major East Asian countries, including China, Taiwan, Japan, Singapore and South Korea, are nearsighted. The overall rate of myopia in the U.K., by contrast, is about 20% to 30%. The research says that the culprit is academic ambition; spending too much time studying indoors and not enough hours in bright sunlight. Certainly this happens in some homes in western countries as well.

Well isn't that a kick in the teeth? Teach your kids to study hard and aim high in school and it hurts their eyesight! What we are talking about here again is balance.

Of course you want to encourage your children to set high standards for themselves, but you also want them to be healthy. Children need sunlight. Indeed everyone needs sunlight, especially those who live in colder climates.

That grandmother was not wrong. For the benefit of your children's overall health, you might want to consider the following. When your children first come home from school, give their eyes a rest and their bodies a chance to stretch. Send them outside to play.

33.

THEIR ACTIVITIES ARE NOT YOURS

Are you a "Dance Mom" or "little League Dad"? Do you take your children to activities and then get so engrossed in those activities that you do not recognize yourself?

No one can fault parents for wanting their children to succeed, to perhaps be the best. Winning instills a sense of pride and accomplishment in both parent and child. And there's the rub.

It is easy for parents to get tangled up in their children's activities, especially if those activities are competitive. You are there for them, not for yourself. If you love competitive hockey and want to do it for yourself, get on a team, coach a team, or get season's tickets and go watch professional games. If you love dancing, take lessons, or go watch some professionals.

It is important to separate your sense of accomplishment from that of your child. Whether the child succeeds or fails in their endeavor is not a reflection of you. The child is there to have fun, and feel good about winning sometimes. But losing a game or having a bad day in a dance competition is not the end of the world. Do not berate the child, the coach or the parents of the other team. Spend your energy teaching your child how to be responsible, accept defeat graciously, and look forward to winning next time.

It is important to maintain perspective. In the bigger scheme of things, demonstrating your love to your child when the child is feeling badly and maintaining open lines of communication between you are what count most.

34.

DEAL WITH YOUR FAMILY OF ORIGIN ISSUES

Family of origin issues are very complex, and they influence every aspect of people's lives. Whether you experienced your family of origin situation as good, bad or somewhere in between, it affects how you relate to your children and how you raise them.

Two people who grew up as children in the same family, and are only a couple of years apart, may raise their children very differently from each other, depending on how they experienced their own upbringing.

One may say they are raising their children exactly as they were raised because they thought that was a good way, whereas the other child may say the opposite and want to raise children very differently.

It really does not matter whether you approve or disapprove of how your parents raised you. And it also does not matter whether you replicate their style or not (providing, of course, that the style you choose does not involve abuse of any kind). What matters is that, if you have issues with your siblings or with one or both of your parents, and have not dealt with these issues, the issues can carry over into your current family.

If you find that you have carryover issues from your childhood, deal with them to the best of your ability. Instead of feeling like a victim and using the words "They did _____", try using the more empowering words "Because they did _____, I feel_____." Then, since you cannot fix the first part of the sentence, you can work on the second. Work on healing your feelings, even if that means getting the help of a support group or a therapist. Then your children will get all of you, free of any potential unpleasant bits of carryover from an earlier time in your life.

35.

BELIEVE IN THEM, NO MATTER WHAT

Parents can sometimes find it difficult to believe in their children. This belief can be particularly challenged if the children have learning or behavioral issues. It is certainly exacerbated during the teen years when almost all children seem to have behavioral issues. No matter how difficult or negative your children may seem, it is important to not let your belief in them waver. Don't give up on them.

People want the best for their children. They want them to succeed and be able to make their own way in life, and perhaps even to be a "somebody".

When children, even adult children, do things that concern or disappoint their parents, it can be easy to lose hope for the child and even write the child off, in other words, cut off communication with that child forever, or at least until the child does what the parent or parents want.

At the base of this mistrust for the children is really the parents' disappointment in themselves. They look at the child and think, "How could I have raised someone like that?" They then cut the child off because they cannot bear to look, not at the child, but at their own sense of failure. They are really angry with themselves, not the child.

In order to continue to believe in your children through the tough times, you have to trust yourself. Trust that you have given, and continue to give all that you can. Trust that you have done your best and that your intentions were honorable. Love them, and trust that, in time, they will find their way. The child with purple hair today could be an upstanding citizen and a paragon of virtue tomorrow. Hang in.

36.

HAVE DINNER TOGETHER, ALWAYS

This piece of advice may seem like an odd one. It was offered by a new grandmother who has excellent relationships with all of her grown children. She is also a very successful businesswoman.

"Dinner time is family time", she said, and recommended that people "move mountains" to make it happen.

Why is having one time each day in which the entire family gets together around one table so important? It gives parents the opportunity to stay in touch with what is going on in their children's lives. As the children get older and spend more time away from home, it is easy to lose touch with what is important to them. You could perhaps even find yourself out of the loop should your children get into trouble.

It is important to not only have dinner together, but to also make dinnertime feel like a safe haven, a retreat from the day, a time when family can relax and be themselves in comfort.

One woman disagreed with this advice, saying that family dinners were torture in her childhood home. If family dinners were unpleasant childhood events that you do not want to replicate, ask yourself what it was about those dinners that was so unpleasant. Perhaps it was mom's awful cooking, but probably not. It more likely had to do with what happened at the diner table. In one family, for example, mother enforced the rule "no talking while you are eating." You can't get updates on what is going on in your children's lives if you do not allow them to talk. Another person said their dad was so grouchy and demanding that family dinners were most unpleasant. Look at what it was that you might not have liked about your childhood family dinners, and ensure that you do differently now.

You may not be able to do family dinners every night because of work or activity schedules, but at least make one night per week family dinner night. Make it safe, and make it fun. See if you can create family dinners to which everyone in the family looks forward.

37.

KEEP YOUR COOL

Losing your cool can have disastrous side effects, especially with adult children. One woman told the story of being terribly upset by her grown daughter's behavior at a family event. She was so upset that she sent her daughter a strong email. Expecting the daughter to be shame-faced and apologetic, the mother was surprised that the daughter was so hurt and upset that she virtually cut off relations with the mother. The tone of the mother's email had been so strong that it overshadowed the content.

There is no doubt that when people are upset, they are not themselves. They are vulnerable to doing and saying things that could damage the relationship. Not everyone is forgiving, and children in particular, believe it or not, have very high standards for their parents. If a thousand people were asked to name something their parents did wrong, there would be no shortage of answers.

So it is important to keep you cool. There will be times when you feel really angry or frustrated with your children. If you are unpleasant to them, either with words or with actions, children can get hurt and they can have very long memories. Every single one of us can remember one thing that our parents did or said, perhaps even when we were very young, which we have not forgotten.

Losing your cool says more about you than about your children. No one makes us lose our cool. No matter what the child does, they are just doing their thing. You are the one who is getting angry. Whatever that adult child did at the family event mentioned above, the mother is responsible for the email she wrote. She is not responsible for her daughter's response, but we can never predict people's responses to our anger. It is best to, rather than worrying about potential responses, manage your anger in the first place. Do whatever you need to do to cool down, and address the issue in a rational manner when you feel better. You will then have a better chance of not only getting the issue addressed, but also of preventing any further damage through misunderstanding.

38.

LIGHTEN UP

When grandmothers look back at the challenges they faced while raising their children, it becomes glaringly obvious that an issue that seemed so critical in the moment, turned out to be no big deal. It resolved itself over time.

Don't take yourself so seriously. There is a story that goes something like this. King Solomon, who is said to have been very wise, asked the royal jeweler to make him a ring with a phrase on it, a few words that would sustain him through difficult times, no matter what he faced before him. The jeweler made the ring for King Solomon. On it was inscribed the words, "And this, too, shall pass."

Parents fret when their children learn to walk late, cut their teeth late, learn to read later than other children, or can't hold a pencil properly. They fret if their children hit puberty too early or too late, or when they begin dating and with whom. They fret over their child's performance in school and their child's ability to choose and prepare for a career. The common word here is "fret".

Children face challenges as they grow up. Some challengers are larger than others. Of one thing there is no doubt; these challenges will be faced with the best of both your ability and your child's. And one way or the other, you will both come out the other side.

What makes the difference when facing these challenges is not necessarily the degree to which the challenge was overcome. Some challenges, for example learning or physical disabilities will be life-long. The key is how you face the challenge.

Lighten up. See each challenge as bump in the road, not the end of the line, and help your child develop tools to continue moving forward.

39.

TREAT THEM AS YOU WOULD AN ADULT

This is an interesting piece of advice. Should we really treat children as we would an adult? If so, what is the advantage?

The person giving this advice suggested that parents should not baby things down for their children. She said that when parents show children respect, they rise to it. Children actually replicate the behaviors they experience.

Threat them respectfully, and they will become respectful. Treat them honestly, and they will become honest. Trust them, and they will become trustworthy. Love them, and they will learn to love. Children do not necessarily become what they are told, they become what they see.

If you show children high standards of behavior, they will demonstrate these high standards. You are their model. They will live what you show them and what you demand of them. They will also live what your tolerate. If you tolerate disrespectful behavior from your children, they will learn that disrespecting you and other adults is acceptable.

So there is a second half to this piece of advice. You not only have to treat your children as you would an adult, you also have to maintain the expectation that they will rise to the occasion, and be willing to compliment them when they do.

40.

HAVE OTHER ADULTS IN THEIR LIVES BESIDES YOU

Some of the advice in this book was solicited from people who do not have children. Their first response when asked for advice on parenting was, "How would I know, I am not a parent?" But they do have valuable advice. They see child rearing from the outside and are not burdened by their own personal perceptions of success or failure. They can often have a more impartial view. They may also be willing to say things that parents would not.

The person who gave this piece of advice was a proud "aunt" to the child of a good friend. She gave the suggestion that children need other adults besides their parents, adults with whom they can talk and perhaps share important information.

This may be scary for some parents, particularly if they want to be in control of what their children learn. Might this other adult fill their child's head with nonsense?

That is where trust comes in. Have other adults that you know well, who share your values and beliefs, in your child's life. That way your child has other adults to bounce ideas off, and you can be more relaxed about the conversations that your child might have in private with that person.

In addition, children can often take advice from other adults that they would be unwilling to take from their parents. When they reach their pre-teen years, children start to rail against parental advice. Even if they know in their hearts that the advice is good, they may reject it just because they need to assert themselves. With a favorite aunt or uncle, the need diminishes.

Sometimes a family friend or relative, with whom the child is close, can be there in serious times when you may not be able to. One person, who does not have children of her own, spoke of how she recently spent months helping an adult nephew out of a difficult situation. The mother had tried but without success. The aunt, however, was able to save the nephew from unmitigated disaster.

Have other trusted adults in your children's lives. You never know when they can come in very handy. Everyone benefits; the children, the other adult, and of course you, too.

41.

USE AGE-APPROPRIATE COMMUNICATION

Sometimes it can be difficult to know the level of communication your child is ready for. A simple example is when a three-year-old asks where babies come from, the answer "Mommy's tummy" is sufficient. This answer will, of course, not do for a ten-year old.

Another example we can learn from is the recent research on children's lying. In a study published in Developmental Psychology, the authors described research showing that "children as young as two years old were capable of spontaneous lying and that lying behavior rose dramatically by the time they were three." Children at this age lie to avoid getting into trouble, but they do not have moral judgment yet. They do not understand that it is wrong to lie until they are around five years old.

Parents should therefore be careful not to have unrealistic expectations of their children's communication skills. Young children can appear more capable that they actually are. Three year olds who steal an extra cookie know that taking the cookie is against the rules. But they think it is fun and feel proud of themselves that they got the cookie anyway. They think it is funny to tell mommy they did not do it. Of course the parent will tell the three-year old that it is wrong to lie, and then give a (hopefully short) discourse on morality. The child may pretend to be contrite, but the child really doesn't get it yet.

At the other end of the spectrum, pre-teen and teenage children expect adult answers. As young as ten years of age, they can be spoken to as adults and they will understand. Answers intended for younger children will only anger them.

Appropriate communication strategy is particularly important with adult children. One woman jokingly recalled how when holding her third grandchild for the first time, her daughter reminded her to support the child's head. Adult children go through a stage in which they do not believe their parents know very much. This requires a different kind of communication. Parents need to let adult children take the lead and find their way. If parents dare to treat adult children like children, there can be dire consequences. Let them create the depth of relationship they can handle from you, while ensuring that they continue to treat you with respect.

42.

BE SENSITIVE TO WHO THAT PERSON IS

"That person" referred to in this piece of advice is your child. There will be times when you will not recognize him or her. It is absolutely astounding how different children can be from their parents.

People only see the world through one pair of eyes, their own. It can be difficult to comprehend how differently other people, even your own children, can approach the same situation.

If you have a disagreement with your child, the traditional response is often to try to convince the child that he or she is wrong, but this may not be the case. Perhaps you are both right. You are just seeing the situation from different perspectives.

Be a scientist, not a judge. Seek to understand where your children are coming from. What makes up their personality? What drives them? Why do they respond in certain ways to certain situations? And honor that. They have a right to see things differently. They have a right to approach things differently. In addition, they will have different skill sets from you. You may be great at languages, whereas they may be great at math. Neither of you is stupid, just different.

Take responsibility for ensuring that you are sensitive to who your child really is, and are okay with the fact that the child may be very different from you.

43.

ALLOW FOR MISTAKES

It is important to cut your children some slack. People learn from mistakes, whether the errors are big or small. Of course you want to have high standards for your children, but it is important to allow them to be wrong once in a while.

A few people spoke of having had perfectionist parents who expected them to do extremely well in everything they did. Some were able to live up to their parents' standards, but others were not. All agreed that the fear of making mistakes or getting things wrong caused them a great deal of stress in their lives.

Some people, who experienced hard-driving parents, replicate this behavior with their own children. They believe it worked for them, so why not for their children. Others take the opposite extreme, not wanting their children to grow up with as much stress as they did.

Find the balance. Too much of a hands-off approach is not good either. Your children need to know that you care about their success. The challenging part is to be able to encourage their success, reward them when they do well, and yet be gentle when they fail. Trial and error is part of growing up. People's most challenging experiences are often the ones they learn from the most. Failing at something or making mistakes feels bad enough without any additional guilt from loved ones. Be the one to pick your children up when they fall, and encourage them to try again and succeed the next time.

44.

BE SUPPORTIVE YET STRICT

A young woman of twenty-three provided this piece of advice. She is not married and has no children of her own, so she spoke from the perspective of an adult child still living at home. She said she was very close with her father but not with her mother. When asked why, she stumbled a bit, then her face broke out into a big smile.

She started by saying that her father is quite strict, but then she smiled further and said that he is also supportive. He is not afraid to say I love you. He would stop in the middle of his workday just to bring her a chocolate bar at her new job. He knew that there was a time to have fun and a time to be serious, and he seemed to be able to blend both in a way that was very endearing to his daughter.

Again the essence is balance. Being too strict can create a home full of stress. Being too fun-loving can create a home without goals and standards. The beauty of this advice is to remind parents that it is okay to act like a kid sometimes, to do spontaneous things that show children that they are loved. As long as you don't embarrass them (because we all know that teenagers embarrass easily) blending strictness with support, love and fun is a winning combination.

45.

DON'T TEASE THEM

Some people think that teasing is just good old-fashioned fun. Others think it helps to toughen children, especially boys, since they will probably have to endure teasing in the locker room if they play team sports.

Teasing is one-sided fun. It is only fun for the person doing the teasing. For the person being teased, it is no fun at all! As a matter of fact, in harassment prevention courses, teasing is listed as a form of abuse.

When a parent teases a child, it is usually a disguised way of telling the child that there is something about the child that the parent does not like. For example, in one family the father is very sporty. From a very young age, the son was sporty, too. But he was also sensitive. The natural response from the well-meaning father was to tease the boy and call him a sissy. He was trying to toughen the child up. He thought the child would find it funny and begin, over time, to be less sensitive and able to laugh it off when he was teased rather than feel offended and start to cry.

In another family, the father is a PhD mathematician, whereas his son is great in sports, yet terrible in math. The father teases the son for being "a dumb jock".

But were being sensitive or "a dumb jock" problems for the children or for their fathers? This harkens back to an earlier piece of advice about seeing your children and honoring them for who they are.

A father may prefer that his son be less sensitive, and another may prefer that the son be better at mathematics. Unfortunately (or perhaps fortunately) children will be who they are. It would be nice if something as simple as a little teasing could change that. There are other ways to encourage your children to become interested in the things that interest you, ways that could be fun for the child, too.

46.

LEARN TOGETHER

When asked for her best advice on parenting, one mother brought up a parenting challenge that she is facing right now with her eight-year-old daughter. It's not even "Do as I say, not as I do," she said, "I don't even know what to say! How do I help her if I don't know how to do it myself?

"I am trying to make her a better person than I am", she went on, "But she is just like me." Her advice was "Your kid will turn out just like you, so be careful!"

The problem that this woman was referring to is that she is a "collector". She has trouble sorting things and getting rid of items that she does not need. She used the example of her night-table drawer. She said, "My night-table drawer is so full, I don't even know what a clean night-table drawer would look like. My daughter's night-table drawer has tons of stuff, too. How do you teach someone to do something that you don't know how to do?"

After a little brainstorming, the young mother came up with some answers for herself. She decided to make it a project to learn to de-clutter together. They were going to invite another adult, perhaps Grandma, an auntie or one of mom's friends to help. They would choose one project and do it together; for example, on Sunday afternoon, Auntie could come over and teach both of them to organize their night-table drawers.

So the real piece of advice here is to not be shy to get help. Everyone has areas in which they are not proficient. It is very common for children to need help learning things that are out of the range of their parent's skill set. Get the support of family members, one of the child's friends, or one of your friends. You might even hire a tutor.

Another aspect to the problem being discussed here is that the mother has an added layer of stress. She is concerned that her child has acquired one of her bad habits, and she blames herself. It is wise to avoid going down that road. Everyone has habits they do not like, and yes, your children may acquire some of them. Take the energy you are spending on feeling guilty and refocus it into finding help for both of you. Learn together and you will solve two problems at the same time.

47.

CHOOSE YOUR BATTLES

"Too many parents make too big a fuss over the little things", said a young grandmother. "If I could do it over again", she mused, "I would worry less."

Young parents think that everything is important. They will bother a little girl about having messy hair when she is playing around the house. Everyone has messy hair when they are hanging out at home; even the little girl's mom has messy hair. The little girl is busy playing with her dollies, who cares about her hair? She'll brush it later.

The teenager's messy room is another one that gets parents upset. Some of the tidiest, well-organized children end up with messy homes as adults, and vice versa. Frankly, who cares? If they want to live in a mess, let them. The day will come when they can't find their underwear and they will learn that they have to keep organized.

It is important to identify what is important in your children's lives and fight for those things. Developing talent and skill is important. Education is important. Finding a career is important. Obeying the law is important. Behaving morally and respectfully is important.

Messy hair? Messy room? Clothes that don't match? Big deal! If your children want to wear two different shoes, Batman capes and green bows in their hair to go to school, so what?

Perhaps this woman's advice is ridiculous, but perhaps she has a point. People see too much of what their children do as a reflection of themselves. If their children dress oddly, they think that people will judge them as poor parents. They also worry that their child will experience ridicule.

Do not underestimate the power of ridicule. It can work in your favor. One woman told the story of her teenager's hair experience. While living in Canada, the seventeen-year-old participated in a fundraiser entitled "Cops for Cancer". The police and various high school students across the city collected money for cancer research from family and friends based on the promise that they would all, in support of people facing cancer, shave their heads on a certain day. The daughter raised over $200 and consequently shaved off her long curly locks. She felt proud and really cool, in more than one sense of the word. Then the family moved to California.

The well-behaved, well-mannered, community-minded seventeen-year old with a shaved head entered twelfth grade. People were afraid of her. Because of her shaved head, they automatically assumed she was a troublemaker and treated her as such. You never saw a child grow her hair out so fast! For one last hurrah, she dyed it purple for Halloween. Mom made no fuss, and even paid for the hairdresser. This washed out after a few weeks, and that was the end of the hair sagas. That teenager is now a responsible, married homeowner in her mid-thirties, who has kept her hair long ever since. Choose your battles! Some of them just do not matter in the long run.

Don't waste your time worrying about little things and silly fads. They pass. Children grow up, they smarten up, and they will surprise you with how much they have learned from you that you never realized.

48.

MAKE THEM INDEPENDENT

The umbilical cord is cut quickly at birth, but the attachment between parent and child is more like a multi-conductor cable, a sheath with many different colored wires inside. These wires get cut one at a time, starting virtually at birth. Is there an age when the emotional umbilical cord between parent and child is truly severed? Who knows?

Independence happens in stages, one tiny step at a time; learning to feed themselves, learning to walk, going off to school, and going off to college. True independence comes when children are able to make important decisions for themselves. Decision-making can be taught, and then the child has to be trusted to make a good decision and be left alone to do so.

Serious letting go happens when a child makes college or career choices. If you make the choice for them, or push them in a specific direction, it can backfire. Here is an example of a parent who could not let go.

Steve loved science in high school, particularly biology, and he decided he wanted to be a doctor. His father was an engineer and wanted Steve to follow in his footsteps. Stepping back, one can clearly see the difference between medicine and engineering. One involves working with living, breathing people, the other with machinery. Passion for one of these careers is very different from the kind of passion required for the other.

Steve went into medicine and was very successful. His father never forgave him. He never took pride in his son's accomplishments, forever admonishing him for not becoming an engineer. Pity! The father's attitude drove them apart, when they could have continued to share a strong father-son bond, even though they pursued different careers.

Teach your children how to make decisions and then let go. Let them make their important life decisions for themselves and support them whatever they choose. If it turns out to be a wrong decision, support them still, guide them as they make a new decision, and resist the very strong temptation to say, "I told you so". Be there and they will come to you when they need you. That is what parenting is all about.

49.

BUILD SELF WORTH

Children need to know that they are important; that the world is a better place because they are here. How can we teach them that?

We are not talking about self-esteem, in which the children feel good about themselves, or self-confidence, in which the children feel good about their ability to do something. We are talking here about something much deeper. We are talking about their mere existence.

No matter how much you help your children develop their talent and skill, and no matter how well they do in school, or how many friends they have, they can face painful challenges that you may not see.

Children need to have such a deep sense of self worth, of their own importance, that if key things in their life fell apart, they could weather the storm.

Feeling of importance can be nourished in a variety of ways, depending on the parents' personality and belief systems and the personality of the child. We spoke earlier of the child who was failing in school, athletics and relationships, whose mom built her self-esteem by making her Mister Fix-it at home. The role had the secondary advantage of increasing her self-worth. She now felt indispensible at home. Without her, who would change the light bulbs and help Mom with the many other needed repairs. It may have been a heavy burden for a nine-year old, but the child knew she helped keep the roof up, and it probably saved her life.

An adult child told of how her mother had unknowingly prevented her from committing suicide when she was thirteen (Imagine!). Her mother used her belief system to help the child see through the darkness. The child was having trouble with the academic and bullying challenges she was facing at school. Even changing schools did not help, and the child was still despondent. Mom's belief system included the concept that we all come into life with a "to-do list" of personal growth challenges that we have to grow through. If she died now, she would just have to do it all over again in a different lifetime, one in which she might be more disadvantaged than she was now. Faced with the knowledge that she would have to learn these things anyway, the child decided to shoulder on. She knew that this lifetime was important, that she was important, and that growing through these challenges was part of the deal.

There are other ways to let children know they are important. Say that you love them often, and prove it. Show them you are proud of them, and that they are necessary in your life. Show them that they are necessary in their extended family's life. Show them as often as you can that the world is a better place because they are here.

50.

HAVE FUN

Being a parent is not jail time, though it may feel like it sometimes. Parents can get so caught up in the day-to-day incessant grind, that they can forget to have fun. Most parents are struggling to keep their heads above water mentally, emotionally, physically and financially.

Stop, take one hour, and go fly a kite. Throw a ball back and forth with your kid, or play some video games and let the child win once in a while. Watch a movie or dress up like geeks and go out for ice cream sundaes.

Add a little crazy fun to your serious parenting. A grandfather of six was reminiscing about his own father. His father had worked hard, including many late nights, to earn a good living for the family. He was a serious man who encouraged his children to work hard, go to university, get good jobs, own homes and make good lives for themselves. Although the son is very grateful for all the good things his father instilled in him, he lamented, "He never once played baseball with me, or came to any of my football games."

The son, now a grandfather himself, may sound ungrateful but let us look at what is gong on here. Think of a person as having three key areas: head, heart and soul. His father did a great job of nourishing the child's head. Tossing a baseball, and attending football games would have nourished his heart and soul, too.

Having plain, good old-fashioned fun with your children nourishes them in ways deeper than you can imagine, and it nourishes you, too. So get up, get out and go play!

CONCLUSION

Parenting is an ongoing learning process that involves being on a constant journey of discovery, and knowing that there is no such thing as perfection. All you can do is your best, and that is all that anyone could ask. It is important to remember to not be shy to ask for help when you feel out of your depth. There are many trained professionals available to help parents and children through difficult times.

The advice in this book is by no means an exhaustive list. It is just a beginning. If you have a piece of advice that you think is important and do not see it in this book, please go to DrSharonletovsky.com and send us an email. We can include it in our newsletter and perhaps even in the next edition of this book.

Happy parenting!

ABOUT THE AUTHOR

Dr. Sharon Letovsky has a PhD in adult education and psychology from the University of Toronto. She is a mother of three and grandmother of four who has been helping people with their personal and professional lives for more than twenty-five years. She writes books, leads workshops and seminars and provides coaching to alleviate suffering and help people be their best.

For information on contacting Dr. Sharon for speaking or coaching, or to learn about some of her other publications, please go to DrSharonLetovsky.com.

www.ingramcontent.com/pod-product-compliance
Lightning Source LLC
Chambersburg PA
CBHW071740040426
42446CB00012B/2406